Soups
& Starters

Rosemary Wadey

D0544101

Gazpacho

Preparation time: about 15 minutes, plus cooling

½ cucumber, coarsely grated

½ small green pepper, seeded and finely chopped

450 g/1 lb tomatoes, skinned

½ onion, peeled

1-2 cloves garlic, peeled and crushed

3 tablespoons oil

2 tablespoons white wine vinegar

1-2 tablespoons lemon juice

2 tablespoons tomato purée

450 ml/¾ pint tomato juice

salt

freshly ground black pepper

To garnish:

thinly sliced onion rings

chopped green pepper

fried croûtons

1. Place the cucumber in a bowl with the green pepper.
2. Liquidize or purée in a food processor the tomatoes, onion and garlic together with the oil, vinegar, lemon juice and tomato purée.
3. Pour the tomato mixture over the cucumber and green pepper, add the tomato juice and mix well. Season to taste with salt and pepper, cover and chill thoroughly.
4. Ladle the soup into bowls. Place the onion, pepper and croûton garnishes in individual bowls and hand separately.
5. Garlic bread or crusty bread and butter make a good accompaniment.

Seafood melon

Preparation time: 15 minutes

2 Ogen or Charentais melons

100 g/4 oz crabmeat, fresh, frozen or canned

175 g/6 oz peeled prawns

150 ml/¼ pint thick mayonnaise (preferably homemade)

grated rind of ½ lemon

½ teaspoon Angostura bitters

1-2 tablespoons lemon juice

To garnish:

4 unpeeled prawns

sprigs of parsley

If small melons are unobtainable, use a large honeydew, cut into either cubes or balls, mix with the seafood, place in small dishes and top with the mayonnaise.

1. Halve the melons, remove the seeds and chill.
2. Flake the crabmeat roughly and mix lightly with the prawns.
3. Divide the mixture between the melon halves to fill the cavities.
4. Combine the mayonnaise, lemon rind, Angostura bitters and sufficient lemon juice to give a thick but pouring consistency.
5. Spoon the mayonnaise over the fish filling just before serving and garnish each with a whole prawn and a sprig of parsley.

Gardener's broth with cheese sablées

Serves 4-6
Preparation time: 30-35 minutes
Cooking time: 45-50 minutes
Oven: 190°C, 375°F, Gas Mark 5

40 g/1½ oz butter or margarine

1 large leek (about 300 g/11 oz), sliced

225 g/8 oz sprouts, shredded

175-225 g/6-8 oz French or runner beans, roughly sliced

900 ml/1½ pints stock (chicken, beef or vegetable)

salt

freshly ground black pepper

1 tablespoon lemon juice

1 teaspoon Worcestershire sauce

pinch of grated nutmeg

300 ml/½ pint milk or a mixture of milk and single cream

Sablées:

150 g/6 oz plain flour

salt

freshly ground black pepper

cayenne

100 g/4 oz butter

75 g/3 oz grated cheese (including part Parmesan)

1 egg yolk

1 tablespoon water

1 egg white or milk, to glaze

sesame seeds

1. Melt the butter or margarine in a large saucepan. Add the leeks and fry gently for 2-3 minutes, stirring frequently.
2. Add the sprouts and beans to the pan together with the stock, salt, pepper, lemon juice, Worcestershire sauce and nutmeg and bring to the boil.
3. Cover and simmer for about 25 minutes or until soft.
4. Cool slightly, then sieve, liquidize or purée in a food processor. Return to a clean pan.
5. Add the milk or milk and cream mixture and bring back to the boil for 2-3 minutes. Taste and adjust the seasoning.
6. Serve with warmed Cheese Sablées.
7. To make the sablées, sift the flour, a pinch of salt, pepper and cayenne into a bowl and rub in the butter, until the mixture resembles fine breadcrumbs. Stir in the cheese. Bind together with the egg yolk and water.
8. Shape into a 2.5 cm/1 inch roll, wrap in foil and chill until firm.
9. Cut into slices 5 mm/¼ inch thick and place on greased baking sheets. Brush with egg white or milk and sprinkle with sesame seeds.
10. Bake in a preheated oven for 10-12 minutes. Cool on a wire tray.

Fennel soup

Serves 4-6
Preparation time: 15 minutes
Cooking time: 40-50 minutes

1 bulb fennel (about 225 g/8 oz), chopped

1 onion, peeled and chopped

900 ml/1½ pints chicken stock

25 g/1 oz butter or margarine

25 g/1 oz plain flour

salt

freshly ground black pepper

1 tablespoon lemon juice

½ teaspoon finely grated lemon rind

300 ml/½ pint milk or a mixture of milk and single cream

sprigs of fresh fennel or chopped fennel bulb, to garnish

1. Place the fennel and onion in a saucepan with the stock. Bring to the boil, cover and simmer until tender, 30-40 minutes.
2. Cool slightly, then sieve, liquidize or purée the soup in a food processor. This may take a little while to get a really smooth purée but it can be left chunky if preferred.
3. Melt the butter or margarine in a saucepan, stir in the flour and cook for 1 minute.
4. Gradually stir in the fennel purée and bring to the boil.
5. Stir in the lemon juice and rind, and plenty of salt and pepper. Cover and simmer for 3-4 minutes.
6. Stir in the milk or milk and cream mixture and reheat gently, bringing back to the boil briefly. Taste and adjust the seasoning and serve garnished with sprigs of fresh fennel or chopped fennel.

Mulligatawny soup

Preparation time: 15 minutes
Cooking time: 1 hour 10 minutes

1 large onion, peeled and chopped

2 carrots, peeled and chopped

2-3 sticks celery, chopped

40 g/1½ oz dripping or margarine

1 tablespoon plain flour

1-2 teaspoons curry powder

1-2 teaspoons curry paste

1.2 litres/2 pints beef stock

1 x 225 g/8 oz can tomatoes

salt

freshly ground black pepper

50 g/2 oz cooked rice (optional)

50-75 g/2-3 oz leftover cooked beef, lamb, pork or poultry, finely chopped or minced

good pinch of ground cinnamon

1. Fry the onion, carrots and celery in the dripping in a saucepan until soft and lightly browned.
2. Stir in the flour, curry powder and curry paste and cook for 1 minute.
3. Then gradually stir in the stock and bring to the boil. Add the tomatoes and plenty of salt and pepper. Cover and simmer for about 45 minutes.
4. Cool slightly, then sieve, liquidize or purée the soup in a food processor and return to a clean pan.
5. Stir in the rice (if used) and chopped meat. Taste and adjust the seasoning and add the cinnamon.
6. Bring back to the boil and simmer for 2-3 minutes.
7. Poppadums make a good accompaniment.

Prawn and pepper chowder with anchovy bread

Preparation time: 20 minutes
Cooking time: 40-50 minutes
Oven: 180°C, 350°F, Gas Mark 4

1 large onion, peeled and finely chopped

2 rashers bacon, rind removed, chopped

1 clove garlic, peeled and crushed

2 tablespoons oil or dripping

1 large or 2 small red peppers, seeded and coarsely minced or chopped in a food processor

225 g/8 oz tomatoes, skinned and chopped

900 ml/1½ pints chicken stock

1 tablespoon tomato purée

1 bay leaf

1 blade of mace

25-40 g/1-1½ oz long-grain rice

1 tablespoon wine vinegar

salt

freshly ground black pepper

50 g/2 oz peeled prawns, roughly chopped

1-2 tablespoons chopped fresh parsley

8 whole prawns, to garnish

Anchovy bread:

100 g/4 oz butter

1 x 50 g/2 oz can anchovy fillets, drained and finely chopped or mashed

1 small French or 1 Vienna loaf

1. Fry the onion, bacon and garlic gently in the oil or dripping in a saucepan until soft but not coloured, about 3 minutes.
2. Add almost all of the minced peppers and continue frying for 2-3 minutes, stirring frequently.
3. Stir in the tomatoes, stock, purée, bay leaf, mace, rice and vinegar and bring to the boil.
4. Add plenty of salt and pepper, cover and simmer for about 25 minutes, until everything is soft stirring from time to time.
5. Discard the bayleaf and mace; add the peeled prawns and parsley. Taste and adjust the seasoning. Simmer for a further 5 minutes.
6. Garnish each bowl of chowder with 2 whole prawns and some of the reserved red pepper. Serve with hot crusty bread or Anchovy Bread.
7. To make the Anchovy Bread, soften the butter and beat in the anchovies. Cut the loaf into slanting slices but leave a hinge on the bottom crust. Spread each slice with anchovy butter and reassemble the loaf.
8. Wrap in foil, enclosing the ends and place in a preheated oven for about 15 minutes.
9. Fold back the foil and serve hot.

Bouillabaisse

Serves 4-6
Preparation time: about 40 minutes
Cooking time: 25-30 minutes

750 g-1 kg/1½-2 lb mixed fish and shellfish (e.g. whiting, mackerel, red mullet, cod, bass, eel, crab, lobster, prawns, crawfish, scampi)

2 large onions, peeled and thinly sliced

1 stick celery, chopped

1 carrot, peeled and finely chopped

2 cloves garlic, peeled and crushed

6 tablespoons oil

1 x 425 g/15 oz can tomatoes or 350 g/12 oz tomatoes, skinned and chopped

1 bay leaf

1 sprig of sage

few sprigs of fresh parsley

salt

freshly ground black pepper

grated rind of ¼ lemon

1-2 tablespoons lemon juice

juice of 1 orange

pinch of saffron or turmeric (optional)

about 300 ml/½ pint boiling water

chopped fresh parsley, to garnish

Traditionally this French dish is made from at least 8 varieties of fish and shellfish but many of the authentic types of fish are only available from the Mediterranean coast. Try a selection of fish and shellfish from your fishmonger after explaining what you want to make. The fish trimmings can be boiled with the water to make a fish stock if liked.

1. Clean the fish, remove skin and any visible bones and cut into pieces about 5 x 2.5 cm/2 x 1 inch. Remove shellfish from the shells.
2. Fry the onions, celery, carrot and garlic gently in the oil in a large saucepan until soft but not coloured, about 5 minutes.
3. Stir in the tomatoes, bay leaf, mace, parsley sprigs, plenty of salt and pepper, lemon rind and lemon and orange juices.
4. Lay all the fish and shellfish in the pan over the vegetables. Add the saffron or turmeric (if used) to the water, then add sufficient of this to just cover all the contents.
5. Bring to the boil, cover and simmer for 15-20 minutes or until all the fish is tender but still in visible shapes.
6. Discard bay leaf, mace and parsley sprigs. Taste and adjust the seasoning.
7. Ladle into soup bowls, sprinkle generously with chopped parsley and serve with plenty of warm French bread and butter. A fork is needed as well as a spoon to eat this soup.

Consommé

Preparation time: 20-25 minutes, plus soaking
Cooking time: 1¼ hours

1.2 litres/2 pints good beef stock

175-225 g/6-8 oz lean beef, minced

1 large tomato, skinned, seeded and chopped

2 carrots, peeled and chopped

1 onion, peeled and chopped

2 sticks celery, chopped

bouquet garni

2-3 egg whites (see method)

shells of 2-4 eggs, crushed (see method)

salt

freshly ground black pepper

1 tablespoon sherry (optional)

few julienne strips of cooked carrot or 25 g/1 oz cooked pasta shapes, to garnish

1. Place the stock in a saucepan with the beef and leave to soak for 1 hour.
2. Add the tomato pulp, carrots, onion, celery, bouquet garni, 2 egg whites, crushed egg shells and plenty of salt and pepper. Bring to almost boiling point, whisking hard all the time, with a flat whisk.
3. Cover and simmer for 1 hour taking care not to break the layer of froth on top of the soup.
4. Pour through a jelly bag or scalded cloth into a clean saucepan, keeping the froth back until last, then pour again through the filter of egg and shells left in the cloth into a clean pan. The resulting liquid should be clear.
5. If not quite clear, return the soup to the pan with another egg white and 2 crushed egg shells. Repeat the whisking, boiling for 10 minutes and straining again.
6. Add the sherry to the soup (if used). Reheat the soup.
7. Place the carrot sticks or pasta in the base of the soup bowls and pour the soup in gently. Serve hot with Melba toast and butter.

Variation:

For a jellied consommé, make as above without reheating and leave to cool. Put 3 tablespoons of the consommé in a basin with 2 teaspoons powdered gelatine and stand in a pan of simmering water until dissolved. Add a little cold consommé to the gelatine, then stir it all back into the rest of the soup and chill until set. (If the stock is weak, use an extra teaspoon of gelatine.) Serve the consommé roughly chopped in soup bowls and garnish with blanched julienne strips of orange rind, or lemon twists.

Moules marinière

Preparation time: 20 minutes, plus opening mussels
Cooking time: 20 minutes

about 3 litres/5 pints fresh mussels

50 g/2 oz butter

1 onion, peeled and finely chopped

350 ml/12 fl oz white wine, dry to medium

150 ml/¼ pint water

2 tablespoons lemon juice

1 bouquet garni

salt

freshly ground black pepper

1 tablespoon plain flour

2 tablespoons chopped fresh parsley

4 tablespoons cream (optional)

For garlic-flavoured mussels, add 1-2 peeled and crushed garlic cloves when frying the onions.

1. Scrub the mussels in several changes of cold water to remove all mud, sand, barnacles, etc. Pull off the 'beards'. All mussels must be tightly closed; if they don't close when given a sharp tap, discard them, for they are dead.

2. Melt 25 g/1 oz of the butter in a large saucepan. Add the onion and fry gently for a few minutes until soft.

3. Add the wine, water, lemon juice, bouquet garni and plenty of salt and pepper and bring to the boil. Cover and simmer for 4-5 minutes.

4. Uncover and add the mussels. Cover again and simmer for 5 minutes, shaking the pan frequently, until all the mussels have opened. Discard any mussels which have not opened, and the bouquet garni.

5. Remove the empty half shell from each mussel and drain off the liquor into a small pan. Keep the mussels warm.

6. Cream the remaining butter with the flour and whisk this beurre manié into the liquor, a little at a time. Increase the heat and boil for 2 minutes. Stir in half the parsley and all of the cream. Taste and adjust the seasoning and pour over the mussels.

7. Reheat thoroughly, then ladle the mussels and their sauce into 4 warmed, large, flat soup bowls and sprinkle generously with chopped parsley.

8. Serve with plenty of hot crusty French bread and butter.

Leek and potato soup

Serves 4-6
Preparation time: 15 minutes
Cooking time: 30 minutes

100 g/4 oz streaky bacon, rind
  removed, chopped

25 g/1 oz butter or margarine

450 g/1 lb leeks, thinly sliced

350 g/12 oz potatoes, peeled and
  diced

1.2 litres/2 pints chicken stock

salt

freshly ground black pepper

1 bay leaf

1 blade mace or pinch of ground
  mace

1 tablespoon cornflour

150 ml/¼ pint single cream or
  milk

chopped fresh parsley, to
  garnish

1. Fry the bacon gently with no extra fat in a large saucepan until the fat begins to run and the bacon is lightly coloured.
2. Add the butter or margarine and leeks and cook gently for 2-3 minutes, until the leeks are beginning to soften, stirring frequently.
3. Stir in the potatoes, followed by the stock and bring to the boil.
4. Season lightly with salt and generously with pepper, add the bay leaf and mace. Cover and simmer for about 20 minutes or until very tender but the potato is still visible as pieces.
5. Discard the bay leaf and mace. Taste and adjust the seasoning. If a smooth soup is preferred, cool slightly, then sieve, liquidize or purée in a food processor and return to a clean pan.
6. Blend the cornflour with the cream or milk and add to the soup. Reheat and bring back just to the boil. Serve sprinkled with chopped parsley.

Carrot and coriander soup

Serves 4-6
Preparation time: 15 minutes
Cooking time: 45-50 minutes

50 g/2 oz butter or margarine

1 large onion, peeled and
  chopped

450 g/1 lb carrots, peeled and
  diced

900 ml/1½ pints chicken stock

1 teaspoon ground coriander

salt

freshly ground black pepper

2 tablespoons lemon juice

about 300 ml/½ pint milk

snipped chives or fresh
  coriander leaves, to garnish

1. Melt the butter or margarine in a large saucepan.
2. Add the onion and carrots and fry gently for 10-15 minutes, stirring frequently, but do not allow to brown.
3. Add the stock and bring to the boil.
4. Stir in the coriander, plenty of salt and pepper and the lemon juice, cover and simmer for about 30 minutes or until the carrots are tender.
5. Cool slightly, then sieve, liquidize or purée in a food processor until smooth.
6. Return the soup to a clean pan with enough milk to give the required consistency and bring back to the boil.
7. Taste and adjust the seasoning and serve hot sprinkled with snipped chives or fresh coriander leaves.

Creamy onion soup

Preparation time: 20 minutes
Cooking time: 45-50 minutes

50 g/2 oz butter or margarine

450 g/1 lb onions, peeled and sliced

2 rashers bacon, rind removed, chopped (optional)

1 stick celery, chopped

25 g/1 oz plain flour

600 ml/1 pint chicken stock

good pinch of ground mace

1 bay leaf

salt

freshly ground black pepper

300 ml/½ pint milk

1 tablespoon lemon juice

150 ml/¼ pint single cream

To garnish:

crisply fried, chopped bacon, snipped chives or chopped spring onions

1. Melt the butter or margarine in a large saucepan. Add the onions, bacon (if used) and celery and fry gently until soft but not coloured, about 3 minutes.
2. Stir in the flour and cook for 1 minute, then gradually add the stock and bring to the boil.
3. Add the mace, bay leaf and plenty of salt and pepper, cover and simmer for about 40 minutes.
4. Discard the bay leaf and allow to cool slightly, then sieve, liquidize or purée the soup in a food processor. Return to a clean pan.
5. Stir in the milk and lemon juice, bring back to the boil, taste and adjust the seasoning. Before serving, stir in the cream and reheat to just below boiling.
6. Garnish with the bacon pieces and chives.

Lettuce and watercress soup

Serves 4-6
Preparation time: 15-20 minutes
Cooking time: about 40 minutes

50 g/2 oz butter or margarine

1 small onion, peeled and chopped or 6 spring onions, sliced

1 small lettuce, roughly chopped

1 bunch watercress, chopped

225 g/8 oz potatoes, peeled and diced

600 ml/1 pint chicken stock

salt

freshly ground black pepper

½ teaspoon Worcestershire sauce

2 teaspoons lemon juice

300 ml/½ pint milk

150 ml/¼ pint single cream

sprigs of watercress, to garnish

To serve this soup cold, turn the puréed soup into a bowl, stir in the milk and cream, taste and adjust the seasoning. Cool, then chill thoroughly before serving.

1. Melt the butter or margarine in a large saucepan. Add the onion and fry gently until soft but not coloured, about 3 minutes.
2. Add the lettuce and watercress and continue frying for 1-2 minutes, tossing well to coat in the butter or margarine.
3. Stir in the potatoes, stock, salt, pepper, Worcestershire sauce and lemon juice, and bring to the boil. Cover and simmer for 30 minutes until tender.
4. Cool slightly, then sieve, liquidize or purée the soup in a food processor. Return to a clean pan.
5. Stir in the milk and bring back to the boil. Taste and adjust the seasoning. Stir in the cream and reheat to just below boiling.
6. Serve garnished with sprigs of watercress.

Cream of pheasant soup

Serves 4-6
Preparation time: 15 minutes
Cooking time: 2-2¼ hours

1 pheasant carcass, raw or
  cooked

1.5 litres/2½ pints water

50 g/2 oz butter or margarine

1 onion, peeled and finely
  chopped

40 g/1½ oz plain flour

salt

freshly ground black pepper

½ teaspoon celery salt

¼ teaspoon ground coriander

25 g/1 oz wholewheat spaghetti
  or long-grain rice

150 ml/¼ pint single cream

2 tablespoons chopped fresh
  parsley

fried croûtons, to garnish

For this soup, use a carcass that still has a
certain amount of meat left on the bones.

1. Put the pheasant carcass into a
saucepan and cover with the water. Bring
to the boil, cover and simmer for about
1½ hours. Drain off and reserve the stock.
Remove about 50 g/2 oz of meat trimmings
from the bones, chop or mince and set
aside. Discard the bones.
2. Melt the butter or margarine in a
saucepan and fry the onion gently for about
3 minutes, until soft but not coloured.
3. Stir in the flour and cook for 1 minute.
Gradually stir in 1.2 litres/2 pints of the
stock and bring to the boil.
4. Add the salt, pepper, celery salt,
coriander and broken-up spaghetti or rice.
Cover and simmer for 20 minutes, stirring
occasionally.
5. Add the pheasant meat and cream, taste
and adjust the seasoning. Reheat gently,
bringing back almost to the boil.
6. Just before serving, stir in the parsley or,
if preferred, sprinkle thickly over the
surface of the soup.
7. Croûtons can be either handed
separately in a bowl or sprinkled over the
soup before serving.

French onion soup

Preparation time: 20 minutes
Cooking time: 45-50 minutes

50 g/2 oz butter or margarine

450 g/1 lb onions, peeled and
  finely sliced

1 litre/1¾ pints beef stock

2 bay leaves

pinch of brown sugar

1 teaspoon vinegar

salt

freshly ground black pepper

4 slices French bread

50 g/2 oz Gruyère, Emmenthal
  or mature Cheddar cheese,
  grated

1. Melt the butter or margarine in a large
saucepan, add the onions and fry gently
until soft. Increase the heat and cook
until they turn a rich golden brown, about
10 minutes.
2. Add the stock and bring to the boil.
Add the bay leaves, sugar, vinegar, salt
and pepper, cover and simmer for about
30 minutes. Discard the bay leaves, taste
and adjust the seasoning.
3. Toast the slices of bread, lay on a baking
sheet and sprinkle with the grated cheese.
Put under a preheated hot grill until the
cheese is bubbling.
4. Reheat the soup, ladle it into bowls and
float the cheese croûtes on top to serve.

Sweetcorn and chicken soup

Preparation time: 10-15 minutes
Cooking time: 1 hour 40 minutes

1 chicken carcass, raw or cooked

1.2 litres/2 pints water

salt

freshly ground black pepper

1 bouquet garni

50 g/2 oz butter or margarine

1 small onion, peeled and finely
  chopped

40 g/1½ oz plain flour

½ teaspoon curry powder
  (optional)

1 teaspoon tomato purée

1 x 300 g/11 oz can sweetcorn
  kernels, drained

3 tomatoes, skinned and
  chopped

good dash of Worcestershire
  sauce

pinch of garlic powder

1 small green or red pepper,
  seeded

For this soup use a carcass that still has a certain amount of meat left on the bones. If you don't have a chicken carcass, use 1 chicken portion and 2-3 stock cubes. If a chunky soup is preferred, there is no need to purée it, simply add the pepper and chicken and serve.

1. Put the chicken carcass into a saucepan with the water, salt, pepper and bouquet garni. Bring to the boil, skim well, then cover and simmer for about 1 hour. Stir once or twice during the cooking.
2. Strain off the stock from the bones and reserve 1 litre/1¾ pints. Pick about 50 g/2 oz of the meat trimmings from the carcass and chop finely.
3. Melt the butter or margarine in a large saucepan and fry the onion until soft. Stir in the flour, curry powder (if used) and tomato purée and cook for 1 minute.
4. Gradually add the reserved stock and bring to the boil. Add the sweetcorn, tomatoes, Worcestershire sauce and garlic powder, cover and simmer for 20 minutes.
5. Meanwhile cut a quarter of the pepper into thin strips and finely chop the remainder. Cook both in boiling water for 5 minutes, then drain.
6. If a smooth soup is preferred, cool the soup slightly, then sieve, liquidize or purée in a food processor and return to a clean pan with the chopped pepper and reserved chicken meat. Taste and adjust the seasoning and simmer for 2-3 minutes.
7. Serve garnished with the strips of cooked pepper.

Hollandaise soup

Serves 4-6
Preparation time: 10-15 minutes
Cooking time: 40-45 minutes

40 g/1½ oz butter or margarine

2 carrots, peeled and finely diced

2 onions, peeled and finely chopped

1 stick celery, finely chopped

25 g/1 oz plain flour

900 ml/1½ pints chicken stock

salt

freshly ground black pepper

2 egg yolks

150 ml/¼ pint soured cream

2 tablespoons chopped fresh mixed herbs or parsley, to garnish

1. Melt the butter or margarine in a large saucepan. Add the carrots, onions and celery and fry gently for 5 minutes without colouring, until soft. Stir in the flour and cook for 1 minute, then gradually add the stock and bring to the boil.
2. Add plenty of salt and pepper, cover and simmer for 25-30 minutes.
3. If a smooth soup is preferred either sieve, liquidize or purée in a food processor. Return to a clean saucepan.
4. Blend the egg yolks and cream together, add a little of the soup and then whisk it all back into the soup in the pan.
5. Bring back just to the boil, stirring continuously and taste and adjust the seasoning.
6. Cool the soup, cover and chill thoroughly. Garnish with chopped fresh mixed herbs and serve cold with bread sticks (grissini).

Chilled cream of artichoke soup

Serves 4-6
Preparation time: about 20 minutes, plus cooling
Cooking time: about 40 minutes

50 g/2 oz butter or margarine

1 large onion, peeled and chopped

675 g/1½ lb Jerusalem artichokes

1.2 litres/2 pints chicken stock

salt

freshly ground black pepper

1 bay leaf

¼ teaspoon ground mace

1 tablespoon lemon juice

150 ml/¼ pint single cream

coarsely grated carrot, to garnish

If you are preparing the artichokes in advance, place them in a bowl of cold water with 1-2 tablespoons lemon juice added, to prevent them discolouring. This soup is also good served hot. Simply reheat once puréed, stir in the cream and serve garnished with chopped parsley or chives.

1. Melt the butter or margarine in a large saucepan. Add the onion and fry gently until soft but not coloured, about 3 minutes.
2. Peel and slice the artichokes and add to the pan. Mix well and cook gently for 2-3 minutes.
3. Add the stock, salt, pepper, bay leaf, mace and lemon juice and bring to the boil. Cover and simmer for about 30 minutes or until tender.
4. Discard the bay leaf. Cool slightly, then sieve, liquidize or purée the soup in a food processor.
5. Turn into a bowl, taste and adjust the seasoning and stir in the cream. Cool, then chill thoroughly.
6. Serve garnished with grated carrot.

Curried prawn soup

Preparation time: about 30 minutes, plus cooling
Cooking time: 30-35 minutes

2 tablespoons ground almonds

2 tablespoons desiccated coconut

150 ml/¼ pint boiling water

50 g/2 oz butter or margarine

1 onion, peeled and minced

2 sticks celery, minced

25 g/1 oz plain flour

1½ teaspoons curry powder

600 ml/1 pint chicken stock

2 teaspoons lemon juice

salt

freshly ground black pepper

1 bay leaf

300 ml/½ pint milk

75-100 g/3-4 oz peeled prawns

4-6 tablespoons double cream

To garnish:

chopped fresh parsley

whole prawns

This soup is also excellent served hot.

1. Put the almonds and coconut into a bowl, pour on the boiling water, mix well and leave until cold. Strain off the liquor and reserve, squeezing out excess with the back of a spoon.
2. Melt the butter or margarine in a large saucepan. Add the onion and celery and fry gently for 3-4 minutes until soft.
3. Stir in the flour and curry powder and cook gently for 2 minutes, then add the stock and coconut liquor and bring to the boil.
4. Add the lemon juice, salt, pepper, Tabasco and bay leaf, cover and simmer for 20 minutes.
5. Discard the bay leaf, stir in the milk and prawns and return to the boil for 2-3 minutes.
6. Stir in the cream, taste and adjust the seasoning and cool.
7. Chill the soup thoroughly before serving garnished with chopped parsley and whole prawns.

Minted avocado soup

Preparation time: 10 minutes, plus cooling
Cooking time: 30-35 minutes
Oven: 180°C, 350°F, Gas Mark 4

40 g/1½ oz butter or margarine

2 tablespoons finely chopped onion

25 g/1 oz plain flour

600 ml/1 pint chicken stock

1 large or 2 small ripe avocados

1-2 teaspoons lemon juice

salt

freshly ground black pepper

150 ml/¼ pint milk

150 ml/¼ pint single cream

1½ tablespoons chopped fresh mint leaves

fresh mint leaves, to garnish

Minted bread:

100 g/4 oz butter

1-2 tablespoons chopped fresh mint

1 small French or 1 Vienna loaf

This soup is good served hot, serve it with garlic or minted bread. Garlic bread is made the same way as minted bread but using 2-4 cloves garlic, peeled and crushed in place of the mint.

1. Melt the butter or margarine in a large saucepan. Add the onion and fry gently until soft but not coloured, about 3 minutes.
2. Stir in the flour and cook for 1 minute, then gradually add the stock and bring to the boil.
3. Peel the avocado, discard the stone and chop roughly. Add to the soup with the lemon juice, salt and pepper. Cover and simmer for 5-10 minutes or until tender.
4. Cool slightly, then sieve, liquidize or purée the soup in a food processor and turn into a bowl.
5. Stir in the milk and cream. Taste and adjust the seasoning.
6. Just before serving, stir in the mint and garnish with mint leaves.
7. For a stronger mint flavour, add the chopped mint to the soup 1-2 hours before serving. Minted bread makes a good accompaniment.
8. To make the minted bread, soften the butter and beat in the mint. Cut the loaf into slanting slices but leave a hinge on the bottom crust. Spread each slice with minted butter and reassemble the loaf.
9. Wrap in foil enclosing the ends and place in a preheated oven for about 15 minutes. Serve hot.

Farmhouse pâté

Serves 6-8
Preparation time: 20 minutes
Cooking time: 1¼ hours
Oven: 180°C, 350°F, Gas Mark 4

225 g/8 oz streaky bacon rashers, rind removed

butter, for greasing

175 g/6 oz belly pork, rind and bones removed

175 g/6 oz pig's liver

100 g/4 oz chicken livers

1 onion, peeled

1-2 cloves garlic, peeled and crushed

salt

freshly ground black pepper

½ level teaspoon celery salt

1 egg, beaten

2 tablespoons wine, sherry, cider or brandy

To garnish:

hard-boiled egg slices

cucumber slices

fresh bay leaves

1. Stretch about half the bacon rashers with the back of a knife and use to line the inside of a greased 450 g/1 lb loaf tin.
2. Mince the remaining bacon finely with the pork, livers and onion.
3. Turn into a bowl and beat in the garlic, a little salt, plenty of pepper, the celery salt, egg and wine.
4. Pour or spoon the mixture into the tin pressing well into the corners and fold the ends of the bacon over the top.
5. Place in a roasting tin containing 4 cm/1½ inches water and cook in a preheated oven for 1¼ hours.
6. Remove from the water bath, allow to cool a little, then cover with a weighted plate or block of wood covered in foil to fit the tin. Leave until cold, then cover tightly and chill.
7. Turn out and garnish with slices of egg, cucumber and bay leaves. Serve with toast, crusty bread or crackers.

Cottage and blue cheese dip

Serves 4-6
Preparation time: 10 minutes

1 small onion, peeled

2 sticks celery

1 clove garlic, peeled and crushed

75 g/3 oz blue cheese, crumbled

225 g/8 oz cottage cheese

2 tablespoons thick mayonnaise

1-2 teaspoons lemon juice

salt

freshly ground black pepper

pinch of celery salt

celery leaves, to garnish

This dip is best made 3-4 hours before serving.

1. Liquidize, mince or finely chop the onion and celery.
2. Add the garlic and blue cheese and beat until smooth.
3. Drain off any liquid from the cottage cheese and add to the mixture, followed by the mayonnaise and lemon juice.
4. Season to taste with salt, pepper and celery salt and beat until very smooth.
5. Turn into a bowl and cover with cling film or foil.
6. Serve the dip garnished with a celery leaf and surrounded by a variety of vegetables for dipping, such as carrot sticks, celery pieces, button mushrooms, stuffed olives and a selection of cocktail biscuits.

Chicken liver dip

Preparation time: 10 minutes
Cooking time: 15 minutes

50 g/2 oz butter

1 onion, peeled and finely chopped

1 clove garlic, peeled and crushed

225 g/8 oz chicken livers

1 bay leaf

1 tablespoon brandy or port

3-4 tablespoons plain unsweetened yogurt

salt

freshly ground black pepper

1 teaspoon capers, finely chopped (optional)

sprigs of parsley, to garnish

1. Melt the butter in a frying pan. Add the onion and garlic and fry gently until soft but not coloured, about 3 minutes.
2. Wash and drain the chicken livers thoroughly. Roughly chop them.
3. Add the livers to the pan with the bay leaf and cook gently for about 10 minutes, stirring frequently until tender. Cool slightly and discard the bay leaf.
4. Liquidize or purée in a food processor, adding the brandy or port and then turn into a serving bowl.
5. Beat in sufficient yogurt to give a creamy consistency, add plenty of salt and pepper and mix in the capers (if used).
6. Leave to cool. When cold, add extra yogurt if necessary, then cover and chill until required.
7. Garnish with parsley and serve with a selection of cocktail biscuits, carrot and celery sticks, cauliflower florets, chunks of cucumber and crisps. If preferred, serve the dip in individual pots.

Smoked salmon pâté

Preparation time: about 20 minutes
Cooking time: 2-3 minutes

4 tablespoons dry white wine

1 bay leaf

1 teaspoon crushed black peppercorns

pinch of cayenne pepper

1 tablespoon lemon juice

1/2 teaspoon tomato purée

225 g/8 oz smoked salmon pieces or trimmings

4 tablespoons plain unsweetened yogurt

about 4 tablespoons double cream

salt

freshly ground black pepper

To garnish:

slices of cucumber

slices of lemon

1. Put the wine into a small saucepan with the bay leaf, peppercorns, cayenne and lemon juice and bring to the boil. Boil until reduced by about one-third, then leave until cold. Strain through a fine sieve or scalded muslin.
2. Whisk the tomato purée into the wine liquid.
3. Remove any skin or bones from the salmon, then liquidize, mince or purée in a food processor until smooth.
4. Whisk the wine liquid into the salmon, followed by the yogurt. Beat until smooth.
5. Beat in sufficient cream to give a spreading consistency.
6. Season to taste, adding salt sparingly, if necessary, and pepper fairly generously, and spoon into 4 individual ramekins or dishes, swirling the top with a round-bladed knife. Chill.
7. Garnish each dish with twists of 2 slices of cucumber and one of lemon. Serve with fingers of hot brown toast and butter.

Duck and orange terrine

Preparation time: 20 minutes
Cooking time: about 1 hour 10 minutes
Oven: 180°C, 350°F, Gas Mark 4

1 large duck portion or 225 g/
  8 oz duck flesh including some
  skin and fat

100 g/4 oz lean bacon rashers,
  rind removed

1 onion, peeled

grated rind of ½ orange

2 tablespoons orange juice

1 tablespoon brandy

1 egg, beaten

salt

freshly ground black pepper

1 small clove garlic, peeled and
  crushed

To garnish:

orange slices

little liquid aspic jelly

fresh bay leaves

1. Strip the flesh off the duck portion and then mince finely, once or twice with the bacon and onion in a mincer, blender or food processor.
2. Turn the minced mixture into a bowl and beat in the orange rind and juice, brandy, egg, salt, plenty of black pepper and the garlic until quite smooth.
3. Grease a casserole or terrine dish (about 600 ml/1 pint capacity) and spoon in the mixture, pressing it well down.
4. Cover lightly with foil or a lid and stand in a roasting tin containing 4 cm/1½ inches water.
5. Cook in a preheated oven for 30 minutes, uncover and continue for a further 35-40 minutes or until cooked through. Remove from the water bath and leave until cold.
6. Garnish with slices of orange and pour over a layer of aspic jelly which is on the point of setting. Chill until set.
7. Before serving, add fresh bay leaves to complete the garnish. Serve with crusty bread or hot toast and butter.

Brandade

Preparation time: 20 minutes
Cooking time: 10 minutes

300-350 g/11-12 oz white fish
  fillets, skinned

about 150 ml/¼ pint milk

salt

freshly ground black pepper

1 small onion, peeled and
  chopped

1 boiled potato (about 100 g/
  4 oz)

1-2 cloves garlic, peeled and
  crushed

2 tablespoons olive oil

1½-2 tablespoons lemon juice

3-4 tablespoons double cream

To garnish:

gherkin fans

tomato slices

1. Put the fish in a saucepan with enough milk barely to cover. Season with plenty of salt and pepper. Poach until tender, about 5 minutes (or longer if cooked from frozen).
2. Drain the fish, discard the bones and flake the flesh roughly.
3. Combine the onion and potato in a liquidizer or food processor until smooth.
4. Add the garlic and fish and continue mixing until smooth.
5. Add the olive oil, salt and pepper to taste, 1½ tablespoons of the lemon juice and 2 tablespoons of the cream and mix to give a smooth texture. Add extra lemon juice and cream, if liked; taste and adjust the seasoning.
6. Turn into a dish, cover and chill thoroughly.
7. Garnish with gherkin fans and tomato slices and serve with toast and butter.

Hors d'oeuvre

Serves 4-6
Preparation time: 30-40 minutes, plus marinating

about 175 g/6 oz small cauliflower florets

100 g/4 oz French beans, cooked

150 ml/¼ pint French dressing

40 g/1½ oz long-grain rice, cooked

2 canned peach halves, chopped

25 g/1 oz raisins

1 small onion, peeled and finely sliced

1 tablespoon lemon juice

1 teaspoon chopped fresh parsley

salt

freshly ground black pepper

4 hard-boiled eggs, halved

2 tablespoons thick mayonnaise

½ teaspoon curry powder

2 teaspoons sieved apricot jam

few capers

6 tomatoes

1 x 50 g/2 oz can anchovies, drained

1 teaspoon chopped fresh mixed herbs

100 g/4 oz garlic sausage, thinly sliced

50 g/2 oz salami, thinly sliced

50 g/2 oz liver sausage, cut into 4-6 slices

50 g/2 oz stuffed green olives

50 g/2 oz black olives

1-2 teaspoons French mustard

4 tablespoons soured cream

To garnish:

lettuce leaves

chopped fresh parsley

This dish can be attractively served on 1 large platter as an alternative to the individual dishes. Cook the French beans until only just tender and still slightly 'crunchy'.

1. Blanch the cauliflower florets for 1 minute, drain thoroughly and put into a bowl. Cut the beans into 5 cm/2 inch lengths and add to the florets with 4 tablespoons of the French dressing. Leave to marinate for 30 minutes.
2. Combine the rice, peaches and raisins. Chop 1 tablespoonful of the onion and add together with the lemon juice, parsley, salt and pepper. Mix well. Place in 1 of the hors d'oeuvre dishes.
3. Remove the egg yolks and mash finely with the mayonnaise, curry powder, jam, salt and pepper. Using a large star vegetable nozzle, pipe whirls of filling back into the egg whites. Top each with capers and arrange in a serving dish.
4. Slice the tomatoes and arrange in a separate dish. (The skins may be removed if preferred.) Chop the anchovies and mix into the remaining French dressing with the chopped herbs. Spoon over the tomatoes.
5. Arrange the slices of garlic sausage, salami and liver sausage in another serving dish, rolling or folding the sausages if liked.
6. Mix the olives together and add the remaining sliced onion; put into a serving dish.
7. Drain the cauliflower and beans and turn into another serving dish. Combine the mustard and soured cream and spoon over.
8. Garnish with lettuce and parsley and serve with French bread and butter.

Egg and pâté tartlets

Preparation time: 25 minutes
Cooking time: about 20 minutes
Oven: 200°C, 400°F, Gas Mark 6

100 g/4 oz plain flour
salt
25 g/1 oz butter or margarine
25 g/1 oz lard or white fat
cold water, to mix
Filling:
175 g/6 oz fine liver pâté
50 g/2 oz softened butter
2 tablespoons soured cream
pinch of garlic powder
pinch of ground coriander
freshly ground black pepper
4 hard-boiled eggs, quartered
sprigs of parsley, to garnish

When available, quail's eggs are delicious in this recipe. Hard-boil them for 5 minutes, shell and arrange 3 or 4 eggs in each tartlet in place of the quartered eggs.

1. To make the pastry, sift the flour and salt into a bowl, rub in the fats until the mixture resembles fine breadcrumbs, then bind to a firm but pliable dough with water.
2. Roll out and use to line four 11 cm/ 4½ inch individual tartlet, flan or Yorkshire pudding tins. Trim off the excess pastry and crimp the edges.
3. Bake blind in a preheated oven for 15 minutes, remove the paper and beans and continue for 5 minutes, if necessary, until crisp. Cool on a wire tray.
4. To make the filling, cream the pâté and butter together until smooth, then beat in the soured cream, garlic powder, coriander and salt and pepper to taste, to give a piping consistency.
5. Pipe or spread the filling into the pastry cases.
6. Arrange the quartered eggs around the pâté. Garnish each tartlet with a sprig of parsley before serving.

Melon cocktail

Preparation time: 20-25 minutes, plus soaking

1 large Charentais or Ogen melon or 1 small Honeydew melon

4-6 tablespoons sweet white vermouth

2 grapefruit

100-175 g/4-6 oz black grapes, halved and seeded

sprigs of fresh mint, to garnish

1. Halve the melon and scoop out the seeds.
2. Either use a melon baller to make the flesh into balls or cut into 1-2 cm/½-¾ inch cubes. Place the melon in a bowl.
3. Pour the vermouth over the melon and leave to soak for 1-2 hours, stirring gently once or twice.
4. Halve the grapefruit by cutting in a vandyke fashion. This needs a sharp narrow-bladed knife and the cuts are made in a continuous 'V' shape all round the middle of the fruit. To make the 'V' shape, insert the knife into the fruit at an angle, taking it into the centre of the fruit with each cut. Reverse the angle for the next cut to complete the 'V'. Carefully pull the two halves apart and repeat with the second grapefruit.
5. Ease the grapefruit segments gently from between the membranes of the fruit and place in a bowl; then remove the membrane, leaving a clean shell.
6. Add the grapes to the grapefruit and chill.
7. Before serving, mix the melon and other fruits together. Divide between the grapefruit shells, piling the fruit up in the centre. Pour the juices over the cocktail. If preferred, the cocktail may be served in glass dishes.
8. Garnish each cocktail with a sprig of fresh mint and serve.

Smoked haddock mousse

Preparation time: 25-30 minutes, plus cooling
Cooking time: 10 minutes

225 g/8 oz smoked haddock fillet, skinned

about 150 ml/¼ pint milk

25 g/1 oz butter or margarine

1 tablespoon plain flour

salt

freshly ground black pepper

good pinch ground mace

2 egg yolks

1 teaspoon powdered gelatine

1 tablespoon water

4 tablespoons soured cream

1 egg white

200 ml/⅓ pint made up liquid aspic jelly

To garnish:

slices of hard-boiled egg

sprigs of watercress

1. Poach the fish in the milk until tender, about 5 minutes. Drain and reserve the cooking liquor. Cool the fish, then remove any bones and flake.
2. Melt the butter or margarine in a saucepan, stir in the flour and cook for 1 minute, then gradually add the reserved cooking liquor and bring to the boil. Simmer for 1 minute.
3. Add plenty of salt and pepper and the mace. Beat in the egg yolks, then leave to cool, covering with cling film or foil.
4. Dissolve the gelatine in the water in a basin over a pan of hot water; cool a little, then beat into the sauce.
5. Add the fish and soured cream and mix thoroughly.
6. Whisk the egg white stiffly and fold into the mixture. Turn into 4 individual dishes or 1 larger dish and chill until set.
7. Pour a layer of liquid aspic over the mousses and chill again until set.
8. Garnish with slices of egg and sprigs of watercress and serve with fingers of hot toast and butter.

Fennel and tuna fish salad

Preparation time: 15 minutes, plus marinating time

2 tablespoons olive oil

1 tablespoon wine vinegar

1 tablespoon lemon juice

grated rind of ¼ lemon

½ teaspoon salt

freshly ground black pepper

1 level teaspoon caster sugar

2 tablespoons cream

1 large bulb fennel, trimmed and cut into 1 cm/½ inch pieces

3-4 spring onions, trimmed and sliced

1 x 200 g/7 oz can tuna fish, drained and roughly flaked

4 large tomatoes, quartered and seeded

about 16 black olives

spring onions, to garnish

1. First make the dressing by putting the oil, vinegar, lemon juice, lemon rind, salt, pepper and sugar into a screw-topped jar. Shake until well blended. Then add the cream and shake again.
2. Place the fennel in a bowl with the sliced spring onions.
3. Pour the dressing into the bowl, mix well, cover and leave to stand for 1-2 hours.
4. Just before serving, mix in the tuna fish, tomatoes and the olives.
5. Spoon the salad on to 4 individual plates or into small bowls.
6. Garnish with spring onions and serve with Melba toast and butter.

Crab and egg mousses

Preparation time: 30 minutes, plus setting

oil, for greasing

450 ml/¾ pint liquid aspic jelly

1 x 200 g/7 oz can crabmeat, drained, or fresh or frozen crabmeat, thawed

2 hard-boiled eggs, halved

1 tablespoon thick mayonnaise

salt

freshly ground black pepper

finely grated rind of ½ small lemon

2 tablespoons double cream

To garnish:

lettuce leaves

gherkin fans

1. Lightly grease or rinse out 6 individual moulds or dishes (about 150 ml/¼ pint capacity). Pour in a thin layer of aspic jelly to cover the base and leave to set.

2. Pick out 6 small pieces of claw meat from the crab and set in the moulds with a little more aspic.

3. Sieve the egg yolks and finely chop the whites, then add to the mayonnaise with 4 tablespoons liquid aspic jelly and salt and pepper. Spoon into the moulds and chill until set.

4. Flake the crabmeat and mix with the lemon rind, cream and remaining aspic jelly. Season to taste and spoon into the moulds. Chill thoroughly until set.

5. Turn out the mousses carefully on to plates arranged with lettuce leaves. Garnish with gherkin fans and serve with Melba toast and butter.

Savoury chicken horns

Preparation time: 20 minutes
Cooking time: 25-30 minutes
Oven: 220°C, 425°F, Gas Mark 7

1 x 200 g/7 oz packet frozen puff pastry, thawed

beaten egg, to glaze

Filling:

40 g/1½ oz butter or margarine

1 large stick celery, finely chopped

25 g/1 oz plain flour

200 ml/⅓ pint milk or chicken stock

2 tablespoons thick mayonnaise

1½-2 teaspoons tarragon mustard or French mustard and ½ teaspoon dried tarragon

1 red pimento, chopped

salt

freshly ground black pepper

100 g/4 oz cooked chicken meat, finely chopped

225 g/8 oz green grapes

sprigs of parsley, to garnish

1. Roll out the pastry thinly on a floured surface to about 30 x 11 cm/12 x 4½ inches and cut into strips about 2.5 cm/1 inch wide.

2. Lightly grease 4 large or 8 small metal cream horn tins. Brush the strips of pastry with beaten egg and wind round the horn tins, keeping the glazed side outwards and just overlapping as you wind.

3. Place the horns on a greased baking sheet and cook in a preheated oven for 15-20 minutes until golden brown. Remove the tins from the pastry horns and cool on a wire tray.

4. Meanwhile melt the butter or margarine in a saucepan and fry the celery gently for 2-3 minutes. Stir in the flour and cook for 1 minute, then gradually add the milk or stock and bring to the boil for 2 minutes.

5. Stir in the mayonnaise, mustard and pimento and season well with salt and pepper; allow to cool. Peel, halve and remove pips from 75 g/3 oz of the grapes, then stir in with the chicken.

6. Spoon the filling into the horns and garnish with the remaining grapes and the parsley.

Avocado with piquant sauce

Preparation time: 15-20 minutes

1 large stick celery

1 clove garlic, peeled and crushed

1 teaspoon grated onion

2 large tomatoes, skinned and seeded

2 hard-boiled eggs

1½-2 teaspoons tomato purée

salt

freshly ground black pepper

few drops Tabasco sauce

1 tablespoon thick mayonnaise or whipped cream

2 ripe avocados

few lettuce leaves

pickled walnut pieces or black olives, to garnish

If you wish to prepare the dish in advance (but it should not be done more than 1 hour before serving) brush the cut surface of the avocado with lemon juice, do not add the sauce, and cover each half with cling film. Remove the film and add the sauce at the last minute.

1. Either mince, grate or finely chop the celery. Mix with the garlic and onion and turn into a bowl.
2. Finely chop the tomatoes and add to the bowl.
3. Either coarsely grate or chop the eggs so they are evenly but not too finely chopped.
4. Add the tomato purée, salt, pepper, sufficient Tabasco to give just a 'bite' and mayonnaise or whipped cream to the celery mixture. Then stir in the tomatoes and finally the eggs. Taste and adjust the seasoning, adding extra Tabasco sparingly, if necessary.
5. Just before serving, halve the avocados, remove the stones and peel carefully.
6. Cut each half into slices lengthwise but leaving a hinge at the 'fat' end.
7. Arrange 2 or 3 lettuce leaves on individual plates and spread out each avocado half to a fan shape (dome side upwards) on the lettuce.
8. Spoon the egg mixture over the 'hinge' end of the fan and garnish with pickled walnut pieces or black olives.
9. Serve with hot garlic bread or brown bread and butter.

Cottage cheese and date salad

Preparation time: 15-20 minutes

100-175 g/4-6 oz fresh or preserved dates

4 sticks celery, thinly sliced

1-2 tablespoons snipped chives (optional)

salt

freshly ground black pepper

segments from 2 oranges (see step 2)

finely grated rind of ½ orange

2 tablespoons French dressing

225 g/8 oz cottage cheese

2-3 heads chicory

1 tablespoon lemon juice

50 g/2 oz dry-roasted peanuts (optional)

1 bunch watercress, to garnish

1. Halve the dates and remove the stones. If very large, cut into smaller pieces; place in a bowl.
2. To remove the segments from the orange, cut away all the peel and white pith from the orange using a sharp knife, then carefully ease out the segments from between the membranes.
3. Add the celery, chives (if used), plenty of salt and pepper and the orange segments to the dates. Mix the orange rind into the dressing, add to the salad and toss lightly.
4. Carefully fold in the cottage cheese.
5. Separate the chicory into leaves. Arrange them on 4 small plates and sprinkle with the lemon juice.
6. Spoon piles of the cottage cheese mixture in the centre of the chicory.
7. Chop the peanuts (if using) and sprinkle over the salads, just before serving.
8. Garnish with watercress and serve.

Marinated kipper fillets

Preparation time: 10 minutes, plus marinating
Cooking time: 5 minutes

4 boneless kipper fillets or 175–225 g/6-8 oz frozen boil-in-the-bag kipper fillets

1 small onion, peeled and very finely sliced or chopped

4 tablespoons white wine vinegar

4 tablespoons olive oil

1½ tablespoons lemon juice

salt

freshly ground black pepper

¼ teaspoon finely grated lemon rind

16 black peppercorns

To garnish:

lemon twists (optional)

stuffed green olives

1. If using unwrapped kipper fillets, place on a piece of foil and package so the parcel is watertight by pinching the joins well together. Place in a saucepan of boiling water and bring back to the boil. Allow 1 minute simmering for fresh kippers or 2 minutes if frozen.
2. Remove immediately from the pan, unwrap, drain off any liquid and place the fillets in a shallow dish in a single layer.
3. Sprinkle the sliced or chopped onion over the kippers.
4. Combine the vinegar, oil, lemon juice, a little salt, plenty of pepper, lemon rind and peppercorns in a small pan and bring to a fast boil. Pour over the fillets and leave until cold.
5. Cover the dish securely with foil or cling film and chill for 12-24 hours.
6. Drain the fillets. Serve on individual plates with a little of the onion on top and garnished with lemon twists (if using) and olives.
7. Serve with brown bread or fingers of toast and butter.

Scallops Newburg

Preparation time: 15 minutes
Cooking time: 15 minutes

25 g/1 oz butter or margarine

1 small onion, peeled and finely chopped

10-12 scallops, rinsed in cold water and drained

1-2 tablespoons lemon juice

3-4 tablespoons sherry or Madeira

salt

freshly ground black pepper

2 egg yolks

1 teaspoon cornflour

150 ml/¼ pint double cream

To garnish:

slices of orange

sprigs of watercress

1. Melt the butter or margarine in a frying pan. Add the onion and fry gently until soft but not coloured, about 3 minutes.
2. Cut each scallop into quarters (or smaller, if very large) and the roe into 2 or 3 pieces.
3. Add to the pan and fry gently for about 4-5 minutes, stirring frequently.
4. Add the lemon juice, to taste, the sherry or Madeira and plenty of salt and pepper. Bring to the boil and simmer for 3-4 minutes.
5. Blend the egg yolks with the cornflour then stir in the cream. Add a little of the juices from the pan and gradually stir the cream mixture back into the scallops. Heat gently, stirring continuously until almost boiling.
6. Taste and adjust the seasoning and bring back just to the boil.
7. Serve on a bed of rice. Garnish with orange slices and sprigs of watercress.

Whitebait with devilled sauce

Preparation time: 10 minutes
Cooking time: 10-15 minutes

1 teaspoon French mustard

1 teaspoon made English mustard

2 tablespoons mango chutney, chopped

pinch of cayenne pepper

¼ teaspoon ground ginger

¼ teaspoon garlic powder or 1 clove garlic, peeled and crushed

salt

freshly ground black pepper

2 tablespoons thick mayonnaise

4 tablespoons soured cream

450 g/1 lb whitebait, fresh or frozen and thawed

3 tablespoons plain flour

oil or fat, for deep frying

To garnish:

lemon wedges

parsley sprigs

1. To make the sauce, mix the mustards and chutney together, beat in the cayenne, ginger, garlic, salt and pepper, then fold into the mayonnaise and soured cream. Turn into a shallow dish and cover until required.
2. Wash the whitebait, drain thoroughly and dry in a cloth.
3. Mix the flour with a little salt, and pepper and put in a clean paper or polythene bag. Add the fish a few at a time and shake the bag to coat them evenly.
4. Heat the oil or fat to moderately hot (180°-190°C/350°-375°F), or until a cube of bread browns in 30 seconds.
5. Put some whitebait into a frying basket and lower gently into the fat. Cook for 2-3 minutes until lightly browned and crisp, then drain on crumpled absorbent paper and keep warm uncovered whilst frying the remainder.
6. Sprinkle lightly with salt and garnish with lemon and parsley. Serve with the devilled sauce and thin slices of brown bread and butter.

Smoked mackerel puffs with horseradish mayonnaise

Preparation time: 20 minutes
Cooking time 15-20 minutes

50 g/2 oz butter or margarine

150 ml/¼ pint water

65 g/2½ oz plain flour, sifted

2 eggs (size 2), beaten

salt

freshly ground black pepper

pinch of cayenne

50 g/2 oz mature Cheddar
cheese, finely grated

100-175 g/4-6 oz smoked
mackerel fillets, skinned and
finely flaked

fat or oil, for deep frying

Sauce:

150 ml/¼ pint thick
mayonnaise

1-2 tablespoons creamed
horseradish

1 tablespoon lemon juice

few drops Tabasco sauce

1 tablespoon chopped fresh
parsley

To garnish:

lemon twists

sprigs of parsley

1. To make the choux pastry, melt the butter or margarine in the water in a saucepan and bring to the boil.
2. Add the flour to the pan all at once and beat hard until the mixture forms a ball and leaves the sides of the pan clean. Remove from the heat and leave to cool for 5-10 minutes.
3. Beat the mixture hard and then gradually beat in the eggs a little at a time, until the mixture is smooth and glossy. A hand-held electric mixer is best to use as it incorporates the greatest amount of air.
4. Season the mixture well with salt, pepper and cayenne, then beat in the cheese and mackerel.
5. To make the sauce, combine the mayonnaise with sufficient horseradish to suit your taste, then add the lemon juice, Tabasco and parsley. Turn the sauce into a bowl or jug.
6. Heat the fat for deep-frying to moderately hot (180°-190°C/350°-375°F) or until a cube of bread browns in 30 seconds.
7. Either put the choux mixture into a piping bag fitted with a large plain 2 cm/³⁄₄ inch piping nozzle and pipe 2-2.5 cm/³⁄₄-1 inch lengths of the mixture into the hot fat, or add teaspoonfuls of the mixture to the fat, about 6 at a time.
8. Fry until the balls are well puffed up and golden brown, about 3-4 minutes. It may be necessary to turn some of them with a fork, so that they cook evenly.
9. Drain on crumpled absorbent paper and keep warm uncovered whilst cooking the remainder.
10. Serve the puffs with the sauce on small plates garnished with lemon and parsley or hand the sauce separately.

Omelettes farcies

Preparation time: 15 minutes
Cooking time: 20 minutes

1 onion, peeled and thinly sliced

1 clove garlic, peeled and
  crushed

2 tablespoons oil

1 red pepper, cored, seeded and
  chopped

100 g/4 oz button mushrooms,
sliced

1 x 225 g/8 oz can tomatoes,
  roughly chopped

salt

freshly ground black pepper

½ teaspoon Worcestershire
  sauce

pinch of sugar

4 eggs

8 teaspoons water

little butter or oil, for frying

To garnish:

watercress

black olives or pickled walnuts

1. Fry the onion and garlic gently in the oil until soft, about 3 minutes.
2. Add the pepper and continue to cook gently for about 5 minutes. Stir in the mushrooms and continue for about another minute.
3. Add the tomatoes with their liquid, plenty of salt and pepper, the Worcestershire sauce and sugar. Bring to the boil and simmer for 5 minutes or until most of the liquid is absorbed. Taste and adjust the seasoning. Keep warm.
4. To make an omelette, beat an egg with 2 teaspoons of the water and salt and pepper. Heat a knob of butter in a small frying pan and, when hot, pour in the egg. Cook almost undisturbed, but pull the sides into the centre just once all round as the egg begins to set. Cook until set and lightly browned on the underside.
5. Spoon a quarter of the filling on to the omelette, fold over and slide on to a plate. Keep warm whilst making the other 3.
6. Serve garnished with watercress and black olives or pickled walnuts.

Curried rice with eggs

Preparation time: 15 minutes
Cooking time: about 20 minutes

175 g/6 oz long-grain rice

salt

50 g/2 oz butter or margarine

1 onion, peeled and finely
  chopped

2-3 teaspoons curry powder

1 small red pepper, seeded and
  chopped

freshly ground black pepper

pinch of ground cinnamon

grated rind of ¼ lemon

40 g/1½ oz raisins

50 g/2 oz cooked peas

4 eggs

4 tablespoons single cream
  (optional)

1. Cook the rice in plenty of boiling salted water for 12-14 minutes until just tender. Drain, rinse under running water and drain again.
2. Meanwhile, melt the butter or margarine in a frying pan. Add the onion and curry powder and fry gently until soft, about 5 minutes.
3. Add the pepper and continue for 3-4 minutes, stirring frequently.
4. Stir in plenty of salt and pepper, cinnamon, lemon rind, raisins and peas, followed by the rice; heat through thoroughly.
5. Poach the eggs until just set.
6. Spoon the curried rice on to 4 warmed plates or into 4 shallow dishes, top with the poached eggs and, if liked, pour 1 tablespoon cream over each egg. Serve immediately.

Prawns and mushrooms in garlic

Preparation time: 10-15 minutes
Cooking time: 15-20 minutes

100 g/4 oz butter or margarine

1 small onion, peeled and finely chopped

2 cloves garlic, peeled and crushed

225 g/8 oz button mushrooms

175-225 g/6-8 oz peeled prawns

salt

freshly ground black pepper

2-3 tomatoes, skinned and roughly chopped

1 tablespoon capers, chopped

3-4 tablespoons double cream

4 slices French bread

1 tablespoon oil

sprigs of parsley, to garnish

1. Melt 50 g/2 oz of the butter or margarine in a saucepan and fry the onion and garlic gently until soft but not coloured, about 5 minutes.
2. If the mushrooms are tiny they may be left whole, otherwise cut them in half. Add to the pan and fry gently for 2-3 minutes, stirring frequently.
3. Add the prawns and continue frying gently for 4-5 minutes, stirring continuously.
4. Season well with salt and pepper. Add the tomatoes and capers and cook for a further 2-3 minutes.
5. Stir in the cream and reheat gently, then taste and adjust the seasoning.
6. Fry the slices of bread in the remaining butter and the oil mixed together, until golden brown on both sides. Drain on absorbent paper and place on 4 plates.
7. Spoon the prawn and mushroom mixture on to the fried bread and serve garnished with parsley.

Smoked salmon and asparagus tartlets

Preparation time: 20 minutes, plus chilling
Cooking time: 40-50 minutes
Oven: 220°C, 425°F, Gas Mark 7;
180°C, 350°F, Gas Mark 4

100 g/4 oz plain flour

salt

25 g/1 oz butter or margarine

25 g/1 oz lard or white fat

cold water, to mix

Filling:

175 g/6 oz cooked asparagus spears or canned asparagus, drained

100 g/4 oz smoked salmon pieces or trimmings, chopped

2 eggs

150 ml/¼ pint single cream

3 tablespoons milk

freshly ground black pepper

1. To make the pastry, sift the flour and a pinch of salt into a bowl and rub in the fats until the mixture resembles fine breadcrumbs. Bind to a pliable dough with cold water, then wrap the pastry in foil and chill for 30 minutes.
2. Roll out the pastry and use to line 4 11 cm/4½ inch individual flan tins, rings or dishes or individual Yorkshire pudding tins. Trim off excess and crimp the edges.
3. Reserve 4 asparagus spear heads for the garnish and roughly chop the remainder. Divide between the pastry cases. Lay the smoked salmon over the asparagus.
4. Beat the eggs with the cream and milk and season well particularly with pepper. Pour into the flan cases.
5. Cook in a preheated oven for 10-15 minutes. Reduce the oven and cook for a further 20-25 minutes, until just set and lightly browned.
6. Serve hot or warm, garnished with the reserved pieces of asparagus.

Italian cheese croûtes with tomato sauce

Preparation time: 10-15 minutes
Cooking time: about 25 minutes

8 small slices white bread

butter, for spreading

about 175 g/6 oz Mozzarella
   cheese, sliced

Tomato sauce:

2 tablespoons oil

1 onion, peeled and finely
   chopped

2 cloves garlic, peeled and
   crushed

2 tablespoons tomato purée

1 x 425 g/15 oz can tomatoes

1 tablespoon lemon juice

few drops of Tabasco sauce

salt

freshly ground black pepper

pinch of sugar

Croûtes:

2 eggs, beaten

3 tablespoons milk

oil or butter and oil, for frying

To garnish:

sprigs of parsley or continental
   parsley

1. Lightly butter the bread on one side and sandwich together with Mozzarella cheese to make 4 sandwiches. Press well together and cut off the crusts. The sandwiches may be left whole or cut in half. Wrap in foil or cling film until required.

2. To make the sauce, heat the oil and fry the onion and garlic until soft, about 3 minutes.

3. Stir in the tomato purée, tomatoes, lemon juice, Tabasco, salt, pepper and sugar. Bring to the boil, cover and simmer for about 10 minutes.

4. Remove from the heat, cool slightly and sieve, liquidize or purée the sauce in a food processor. Reheat, taste and adjust the seasoning.

5. Just before serving, beat the eggs and milk together and season well with salt and pepper. Dip the sandwiches into this mixture until just moistened.

6. Heat a shallow layer of oil or butter and oil mixed (do not use more than 75 g/3 oz butter) in a frying pan and fry the croûtes until golden brown on each side, about 5 minutes in all. Drain well and keep warm.

7. Garnish with parsley and serve hot with the tomato sauce.

Spinach and ham stuffed cannelloni

Preparation time: 35-40 minutes
Cooking time: 35-40 minutes
Oven: 220°C, 425°F, Gas Mark 7

4 cannelloni

salt

1 tablespoon oil

Filling:

25 g/1 oz butter or margarine

1 onion, peeled and finely
    chopped

1 tablespoon plain flour

150 ml/¼ pint milk

1 x 225 g/8 oz packet frozen
    chopped spinach, cooked

100 g/4 oz cooked ham, minced
    or finely chopped

freshly ground black pepper

pinch of grated nutmeg

Sauce:

25 g/1 oz butter or margarine

25 g/1 oz plain flour

275 ml/½ pint milk

½ teaspoon made mustard

50 g/2 oz mature Cheddar
    cheese, finely grated

1 tablespoon grated Parmesan
    cheese

Sheets of lasagne can be used in place of the cannelloni. Cook as usual, then divide the filling between them and roll up evenly to enclose it.

1. Cook the cannelloni in plenty of boiling salted water with the oil added for 5-6 minutes, then drain well.
2. To make the filling, melt the butter or margarine in a saucepan and fry the onion gently until soft and lightly browned.
3. Stir in the flour and cook for 1 minute, then gradually add the milk and bring to the boil for 1 minute. Remove from the heat.
4. Squeeze all the water out of the cooked spinach and stir into the sauce with the ham and season well with salt, pepper and nutmeg.
5. Fill the cannelloni with the spinach mixture using a teaspoon or piping bag fitted with a large plain vegetable nozzle. Arrange in 4 greased, individual, shallow, ovenproof dishes or 1 larger one.
6. To make the sauce, melt the butter or margarine in a pan, stir in the flour and cook for 1 minute. Gradually add the milk and bring to the boil for 1-2 minutes. Remove from the heat, season well with salt and pepper and beat in the mustard and most of the grated cheese.
7. Pour the sauce over the cannelloni and sprinkle with the remaining grated cheese and the Parmesan.
8. Cook in a preheated oven for about 15 minutes until bubbling hot and browned, or under a preheated moderate grill until browned.

Potted shrimp pancakes

Preparation time: 20 minutes
Cooking time: 20-25 minutes

50 g/2 oz plain flour

pinch of salt

1 egg

125 ml/¼ pint milk

fat or oil, frying

Filling:

40 g/1½ oz butter or margarine

50 g/2 oz button mushrooms,
   chopped

25 g/1 oz plain flour

150 ml/¼ pint milk

2 tablespoons white wine

1½ teaspoons lemon juice

2 cartons potted shrimps (about
   100 g/4 oz)

salt

freshly ground black pepper

butter, for greasing

Topping:

1 tablespoon Parmesan cheese

40 g/1½ oz Cheddar cheese,
   finely grated

1. To make the pancake batter, sift the flour and salt into a bowl. Make a well in the centre and break in the egg.
2. Gradually add the milk whilst beating in the flour from the edges of the bowl to give a smooth batter.
3. Add a knob of fat or a little oil to a small frying pan and, when hot, pour in sufficient batter to cover the base of the pan. Cook gently for 1-2 minutes until lightly browned, then carefully turn over. Cook the second side until browned and turn on to a plate. Make 3 more pancakes in the same way.
4. To make the filling, melt the butter or margarine in a pan, add the mushrooms and cook gently for 2 minutes.
5. Stir in the flour, cook for 1 minute, then gradually add the milk and bring to the boil.
6. Stir in the wine, lemon juice, shrimps and plenty of salt and pepper and simmer for 2 minutes.
7. Divide the filling between the 4 pancakes and roll up. Place in a shallow, lightly greased flameproof dish.
8. Sprinkle first the Parmesan and then the Cheddar cheese over the pancakes and cook under a preheated moderate grill for 4-5 minutes or until a light golden brown. Do not overbrown or the pancakes will become dry. Serve hot.

Note

1. All recipes serve four unless otherwise stated.
2. All spoon measurements are level.
3. All eggs are sizes 3, 4, 5 (standard) unless otherwise stated.
4. Preparation times given are an average calculated during recipe testing.
5. Metric and imperial measurements have been calculated separately. Use one set of measurements only as they are not exact equivalents.
6. Cooking times may vary slightly depending on the individual oven. Dishes should be placed in the centre of the oven unless otherwise specified.
7. Always preheat the oven or grill to the specified temperature.
8. Spoon measures can be bought in both imperial and metric sizes to give accurate measurement of small quantities.

Acknowledgements

Photography: Bryce Attwell
Photographic styling: Roisin Nield
Preparation of food for photography: Rosemary Wadey
Page 12 Tiles from Sloane Square Tiles, 4B Symons Street, London SW10
Page 14 Bowl from Elizabeth David, 46 Bourne Street, London SW1
Page 18 Tiles from Sloane Square Tiles
Page 30 Plates from Elizabeth David
Page 58 Plate from Elizabeth David
Page 62 Tiles from Sloane Square Tiles

First published in 1982 by
Octopus Books Limited
59 Grosvenor Street, London W1
© 1982 Hennerwood Publications Limited

ISBN 0 86273 039 2

Produced by Mandarin Publishers Limited
Printed in Hong Kong